In Blue And White

one

ombuds sattva

BookLeaf Publishing

India | USA | UK

Made with ❤ on the BookLeaf Publishing Platform
www.bookleafpub.in
www.bookleafpub.com

Dedication

to my friends on facebook, who've taken the time to read some of these poems, and who have expressed some joy upon their reading - here's to aria squire, lexi alexandra, eve reece, sarah bolger, blue whittle, vinay varma, antony mark, little bear, kathryn baranackie, antara roy oruganti, shubha suresh, melissa pariseau, wendy ryan, swagata deb, jane parry, razzya emam dasram, ashish balaya, tod davis, ianup bodge, subhashis sircar, rolf helbig, paromita dasgupta, marian long, mousumi roy, supriya munshi, natalie miller kharchaf, shylo mason, kate dahan, boelo boelens, jamie zabbia, jacinthe malenfant, mack paul, magdalena herzog, julie minton, tom crawley, john villalobos, amit maitra, barb brown, rahul banerjee, robin dale, norma mora miller, shivaji majumdar, latha hn, ravindra k banthia, anil rajadhyaksha, dinakar s manivakam, michael krammer, ani vayu

i am remiss for those i have not mentioned!

Preface

this started off as a blog, at

https://yaopearson.blogspot.com

i started to write a poem a day in 2012, and have so far

written around 56 poems, from which i've picked out 21,

those i think will give pause to the reader, as i meander

through my mind and examine the thoughts that bubble

up, as oft they do.

my word-salad poems are fanciful and i've attempted a

stream-of-consciousness motif: i hope you like the

presentation, as quite a few of these poems were a

cathartic release, and visceral in my writing them

i've called this selection "in blue and white - one" as they

are intended to depict 2 moods, one blue, the other a

scintillating white, that admixture of colors that we so

take for granted as a single color!

hope you enjoy reading these poems, i had quite a bit of

fun writing them!

Acknowledgements

to the sun

moon

the winds

water

fire and aether that are the quintessentials of the
traditional break up of elements (not forgetting the
earth!)

the sun and moon should last the longest, across our tiny
slivers of time that we pluck out to live, out of eternity
and of course, our beloved earth, the mother nature who
gives us birth in her cocoon of a womb, nurtures and
sustains us from one noumenon to the next, the
awesome and bewidering to some, birth and demise

i salute the tribes that we as a human tribe share with
the other denizens of gaia, the plentiful life forms that
are so variegated, and which are responsible for the
unity amongst the simplest of intuition, that predilection
to progress, part of all life

1. in blue and white

in blue and white

and while one's ensconced in the cocoon of the sleep
that's the trance,

the other resumes the nocturnal peregrinations

that seek out mesmer,

swinging from one potential of a place of rest,

to that of the tumbling

sands of dwindling energy sucked by

a personal

pandora:

with her many axes to grind,

as she cleaves through

the dichotomies of the

non-existent colors

black and white

a

blue

hue

instead emerges to take their place,

and now it's the time to wield

a different kind of axe,

to make the music of the blind

singing for reparations

wailing in agony with the screeches

of banshees on valve amps,

the bass is good,

and listening, pinkish membranes

partake of the mawkishness

while all the while,

semi-circular canals

strive to keep the

balance.

rock and roll never had it so good.

2. rain in my heart

as they successfully block our sun - ah these
cumulonimbus with their empty threats of rain
and maybe i spoke too soon? there's the patter of rain
beating tattoos upon the corrugated asbestos sheets that
cover the shed
rain flies arrive from nowhere, busily buzzing around, as
the harsh drops of the water from above beats their
slender wings off - soon, many are crawling upon the
ground, bereft of their flying wings, they hardly seem to
mind their discomfort, happy to explore the floor and
climb up where they can

in the meantime, the skies let up and the now light
clouds grudgingly make way for me to get a glimpse of
azure once more

ah love must surely be in the air as the afternoon breaks,
full of promise.

i've got my blues to listen to, and stuff to read, perhaps a bit, write

who knows what the future has in store for us?
i think i do, and a wee bit, but i'm not telling!

3. four states

the day was long, tiring and fruitful, got a lot of thinking
done, with my pre-frontal cortex chattering away
119 to the dozen, expending 20 watts of power, as 10
percent of my brain saw use
the afternoon, a deep and dense cat nap, with the mental
excursions of distant dreams that somehow felt full and
filling - and a drift off into no-me land, when body
healed myself, ending with some cool REM where i saw
that the stars were a visiting, kinda blissful, with such
peaceful colors and the warmth of oxytocin flooding as
someone i knew hugged me tightly
tis wondrous, the way we traverse our states of being,
conscious, to semi-conscious to un-conscious, such
effortless merges - with insomnia refusing to let us drop
into our unconscious state, when dreams and exciting
thoughts conspire to elevate the "active" mind - happens
seldom these days.
what's intriguing is what's the substratum of the
connection between beings - a continuous presence that
cannot be sensed - there are no "i"s there, nor eyes.

this silent fourth state is the glue of all consciousness,
past and present and future
it's akin to the entire ocean and surrounding atmosphere,
where icebergs of individuality poke out into waking
consciousness, what's below being dream-sleep, with the
lowest part of the berg the autonomous nervous systems
of living beings, when the iceberg heals itself, "coming
up for air" during REM sleep, where the subtle body
"heals"
verily, the ocean includes everything/everyone
and we drift on, forever connected, sometimes not
knowing why and how

4. stardust

the canopy overhead is hidden by the magique of our
sun,
who:
creates the deep blue skies by scattering
the clouds by evaporating waters
heating the airs that carry the white wisps into the
atmosphere's upper reaches
evaporates the waters to impregnate the clouds
causing rain at their whim of heaviness
upon rising, paints the clouds he creates into fantabulous
hues
the brush of his crayons consummate and delicate
and visiting the western rim creates majestic sunsets
his brethren above watch with amusement as he
mesmerizes the denizens upon earth by creating their
circadian rhythms, with the pale moon spinning lustrous
shade come the dark nights, muse and tide maker
the illusion is compleat!
the earth spins and revolves, all under the auspices of the
multitudinous stars above, below, and all around,

ensconced in the brilliant and slow dance, as if in a
burning room
we are cosmic beings under the impression that we are
earth, nay, sun bound
we are stardust!

5. muse mine tonight

every ringlet
of her hair
is touched with the caress of
my breath
that follows the contours
of her mind in mine own
passage of mind,
to find a semblance of
respite and rest
from the officious
inane and the humdrum,
the jetsam of so many more
wills' o' the flotsam;
and after some reduce in
the attendant enervation
in that place with
an absence of battle,
she must but ensue
forth
into the

frenetic, the mislabeled
caricature called 'life'

11

6. going green outside

the evening
washes her
colors over trees
waiting in repose
to catch them
after a day
spent
spinning cool shade
for passers and by-
standers
and soon the dew
will be
upon
grass blades dawning with
the reminder of a sweet
wetness, that
of one
falling, before
spring returns my forest
to its verdant fulness,

the trunks thick with
the sap of summer.

7. madness to the method

the patter-pitter of tiny feet warm something in my heart
the voice a tinkling of a bell
small and dainty in carriage
a bright clean mind
watching ever outward
in trust so much that
makes me want to be more trustworthy
those days flew and passed by my mind's hearing and
sight
strange, that i can still recall them as if they'd happen
tomorrow
so, i close my eyes and count to twenty to be but
transported
to today, at best
what shall i do with my nostalgia for them
and what shall i do for my own nostalgia
whence i was but a boy of peace and contentment
until the time when my heart-strings were tugged by
another
what about that yearning, i feel that too, sometimes,

even when my eyes are open
no, no, i don't fret at all, i have my method: i put these
things next to me, by my side
they sit for a while, and losing interest in my mind, so
calm,
they are driven to boredom and take leave without even
a
word wishing me for the day's start or end, make their
ghoulish exit
only to return once more, sometimes with a renewed
vigor
that scares me none at all:

i start to enjoy my nostalgic yearnings once more.

8. love's embarrassment

the shape of my heart is that of a lover
my blood courses with its music
my fingers tap the staccato of a frenetic blowing
of the mind escaping with a different bass line
ever when the time comes to own up to it
a strange pallor descends upon the countenance of the
loved,
unused to such a display, hence bemused to the point of
a sharp embarrassment
surely this cannot be something
that would bring happiness and joy
so great in love
and such an imbecile in his mundane matters
surely such a thing as common sense
has taken leave here
and has left the scene along with
the laughter and smirks
mawkish following
and onct when the time comes
she will be far away in her heart,

proximal by measured distance
while i will do keep on wondering why i did
what i did
wrong
i don't know the answers to both
as i drift aboard shards of my misdoings,
followed by regrets in a spate of misgivings.
i continue my sojourn after the
transfinities in the meantime, and
my heart is the shape of a lover's

9. kaleidescopic sense

let me walk on eggshells today
and tomorrow too -
balancing atop my fringe a largish lemon
i start with the selfsame something
that i stop without,
my without feels light, now that i've opened my eyes
and
shone my awareness within,
being able to see what
i'd heretofore missed,
a reassuring thing, that I can still feel my voice, my
whisper,
my music of my muses:
now that the 'plane overhead has left peace in its wake,
i can see by listening,
smell by looking;
i must have a JIT engine somewhere,
to provide for a larger tag set and
hence more facets

10. sunburn

the day wore gloomy clouds beset with
a brisk breeze
the moisture in the air
wet my exposed arms
and so it wore on until it
changed its garb for
a light blue
shedding the grays and letting
slivers through of
slender light white while
evaporating wisps of tender cloud
beat it in the sun's face
ah, glorious white,
how well you stand next to your cousin black
never belittling him for his whimsical
lack of color
to be one with our savior who never fails to
keep us warm even if it's but a little
a god doing his duty
so we may do ours

the days bless us to do our bidding
the night to comfort tired souls in its cocoon of fuzzy
dreamland,
antioxidants vs freeradicals in subdued cadence

11. and to us, our little selves!

ensconced in the cocoon of relative comfort
oblivious to deja vu, unaware of naught else
but the sounds of his vainglorious coloring
his lenses purple: he was struck by a thought,
(what an accident!), that he thought would assuage the
gnawing at the pit of his visceral being, rent asunder
by a dismal guilt at the promises he'd balked at to keep
In soliloquy, he mumbled, 'i have to make peace with
myself so that i can make peace with the world'
let the bygones lie, like a sleeping dog content with his
bellyful of the choicest meat-eats, he even made snoring
sounds.
random ramblings brought about by this fight to stave
off sleep, a tenuous drawing into the stretched fabric of
time
my cares may be many, yet i have no cares left with her
in my heart, subsuming every step i make,
circumscribing my existence within the warmth of her
being

and boy, does she shine, as only she can
an effulgence that dissolves my boundaries
makes me whole, makes me want to remake myself ...

12. sap unheard

there's this visceral sleep-inducing-weight
a strange torment, maybe an evisceration may rescue
the
rest of the innards
amazing things, what we call our bodies, and the mind
that encompasses them, through our sleep
and without
i put to rest one, another clamors for attention upon
waking
pesky, the only way out is through kempt rooms of
thought
drift like wood, jostling with the semi-finished flotsam
that seeks a-finishing, can come undun when left that
way
at this point, i put down this figurative pen of mine and
wonder in my forest: forget myself, can anyone outside
hear?
Apparently they can as their mind's pendula swing back
and forth my being myself.
(Yikes!)

13. in motion

an apparition stole part of the night
in anticipation of mirth at its expense
the gloaming called incessant
the cheerful budgie in its roost
comfort becoming of the warm confines
of hay that had seen its heyday
almost chewed into cud
but cleverly whisked away by the pitchfork making
signatures of 8 in its wake on its way to better places
random mutations fit perfectly into fractal shapes
as the curves moved, forever continuous
yet never ever differentiable

14. conceit, mine!

golden orbs of empty silence pause to punctuate the
evening darkness with their gonging
she lies await to the throngs of those who must not
forget
to remember her grandeur,
her power,
her grace,
her compassion,
her divinity,
ever forgiving of her children who forsake her for
nigh on 355 days
spending those days in the
drunken stupor of the fullness of
themselves
as if from post to pillar they run
uncentered around the reason for their
existence
as for me,
i approach her to remove my handcuffs of
ignorance

she smiles as she unfetters me
i ask for the boon of learning
which she bestows upon me
mirthful at my childishness
she is the
origin,
the continuous
mother
of everything

15. free willy

an elastic boomerang switches direction to fly elsewhere,
who says that only humans can exercise freedom of
volition?
the nightingale sings a different tune to different
audiences,
what's to say that she knows but worse

notwithstanding pavlov,
a dog waves his tail upon seeing his master,
a creature of happiness at every such occasion
and a family of ducks cross the road,
swear to god,
at no other place but at the designated 'duck crossing'
sign
as do the deer,
getting all so demure in the presence of men, vehicle,
and in frozen motion upon being blinded by headlights

'tis only a human, then, who,
with all the volition they can muster,

fall prey to habits of deed,
of thought,
of deeply rutted epiphany,
myopic, narrow mindedness and bigotry
casting aspersion upon everyone else but themselves
these byproducts of being drunken with the power of
'free will', unworthy in its reign,
unbridled mongering after power and riches,
paying no heed to the destruction they wreak in their
wake,
as if they are entitled to everything they lay their eyes
on
and forgetting that we are all born animals,
with but the capacity to become human over lifetimes
individual

16. ...hope it's her, not him?

and then i saw the lone reaper
with my own ears,
and heard him with
my eyes: looking straight at me, he knew my time
had come.
nothing wicked there,
just a calm assurance that was good for confidences,
a shared anecdotal episode,
no morbidity, too, just a quite a quiet appraisal of each
others'
countenances
not cold, numb nor sordid:
only, the world around starting to
move with the purpose of meeting with
the persona,
the only one that matters,
shining through fogs' clouds,
warming at a distance, action at some more.
what heralded the reaper were simple things:
was the time spent well,

did the evolution spell at all, was there any?
So a rambling upon the
blue abyss of the sky but
settled on those delectable puffs of
wet disdain until they became
denatured water,
the mainstay of life.

17. picnic basket

the stork carried a stocking-stuffer filled with the black
raven's eggs, waddling on webbed feet for part of the
way - the stocking was heavy and the sticky mud slimy
didn't help any
a skeet shooter came across this ambling denizen of the
swamp, and thought he may be lucky within a few
potshots
robbing her of the rest of her life for a pleasure small
surprisingly, he stopped short, in the taking-a-shot
stance
some strange hand clutched his heart and squeezed to
his perturbation
this had never happened to him, ever: yet that
persnickety feeling connected him to a compassion that
he was hitherto unaware of. for seconds he was
transformed into a human being, desirous of
communion, with that which is within and that which is
without
he felt a freedom in his limbs, his voice was unfettered
in his glorious utterance of tranquil soliloquy, unable to

believe that his mind could experience such freedom
and the stork? the stork walked by blissfully unaware of
what had just transpired.
or was she?
i couldn't tell by her demeanor

18. touching kiss

while a tendril of
hair
gently tumbles
down
to whisper a caress
onto her cheek,
i sit by and gloss over
a magazine describing
a plasma burst on one end of
andromeda:
ah, I've missed that again,
just like I missed watching
the dew drop that kissed
the earth,
while ambling down the two blades of
grass that bent down to let it
utter sweet somethings
onto their skin during her descent
last morning

19. an episode in the morning :-)

my trinkets are all a-broken,
they fell pall-mall to the floor
as i watched the green lawn glisten with the
dew of the morning
my customary black bird fussed in only the
noisy way she can
while two squirrels' pretense at immobility was comical
beyond their bright dark
eyes
a few crows cawed in the periphery, it promised to be a
desultory day
if still waters are deep, the still air promotes a myriad
flies'
sultry-settle on moist bushes
the tendrils of a creeper wait like the parasite it is to
intertwine
itself around whatever it is that's closest
an uncalled for tear found its way past the
crevice of the sinus to settle in a nook by the upturned

smile,

salt and all

the moat of my mind is being cleansed today:

tomorrow will find it in repair

under the drawbridge of

my understanding

and yet the effulgent eludes me,

i can only but wish for some grace to descend,

give succor, and dance me away into the warmth

of the cocoon of my finite bliss:

so wait i shall

20. respite

a silent retreat into the land of no qualms
where serenity isn't the ennui of things to fill the mind
incessant chatter, soliloquacious(!) debates demanding
volte face
it's a glimpse into a facet that is of passing interest to me
the rubric of a woven fabric as garb would have it
stretched across my imagination, taut in expectation
no inanities that bother, the gnawing at an old wound
stops
the magic of simplicity is but skin deep, rhetoric be
damned
the devil take no one, this one's on me
having long hung up my hang ups, there is
yet peace that brings itself to bear upon
an impatience unfounded
As taxi drivers are wont to say, 10-4, over and out
the wafting zephyr under my jacaranda of sorts grazes
past an anticipatory cheek, shade is good, it soothes,
offering some

respite

in the summer sun

37

21. the veracity of falsehood

we speak in tongues,
each mood a language in its own right
we feel blue, sometimes, and red, perhaps?,
at others
sometimes our talk has the ulterior motive of a
one-up on the other
yet at other times we speak the truth, of course,
only as we know it
because anything others say becomes falsehood
even before its utterance
so we are our own - and intelligent - bundle of
prior judgement when
we can only understand something through the lenses
of
our combined and current understanding
it's not entirely untrue that we atrophy along
the lines of our opinionation,
(if that's even a word!),
those of us who've skirted such 'choices' to be made in
life

are blessed with
a modicum of sanity not accruing to the rest of us
i prefer deferred understanding
because it's worked for me
plus, i've heard that i'm dense,
in certain quarters,
whilst in others i'm looked upon with
some regard
Personally, i don't mind
being dumber than anybody else